POLITICAL REALISM

Dedicated to Sixtine Jeay and Bastien Frimas

POLITICAL REALISM

PRINCIPLES & ASSUMPTIONS

ANTOINE DRESSE

ARKTOS
LONDON 2025

ΛRKTOS

Arktos.com fb.com/Arktos arktosmedia arktosjournal

Le réalisme politique published by La Nouvelle Librairie éditions in 2024.

The series Foundations is the result of a cooperation between Arktos Media and the Institut Iliade (Paris). The French original is published in the series 'Collection Longue Mémoire de l'Institut Iliade'.

ISBN
978-1-917646-45-1 (Paperback)
978-1-917646-46-8 (Ebook)

Translation
Roger Adwan

Editing
Constantin von Hoffmeister

Layout and Cover
Tor Westman

CONTENTS

꿎

INTRODUCTION

I T I S A Q U I T E widespread prejudice to believe that good ideas are indeed sufficient to give rise to good politics. The connection between the two seems obvious: politics is defined as a set of decisions made with the aim of putting certain ideas into practice. As for the idea in question, it is the 'object' of the policy that the latter sets out to achieve, and the fact that the policy itself often acts in contradiction to the initial idea is said not to be a source of serious objection. One thus simply blames the flawed nature of our world and the tragedy of human existence, but in no case does one question the importance of the idea as a means to actually impact reality. Now, everyone has their own ideas, of course, and those interested in politics even more so, yet this alone does not render them *political*.

The relationship between politics and ideas is, in fact, not as simple and direct as it appears, for the term 'idea' encompasses several meanings that should be distinguished from one another and kept in mind, so as to correctly analyse the very nature of this relationship. As Ernst Niekisch[1] rightly points out, an idea can be first understood as a *moral require*ment, an *ethical norm* or a *duty*. In such a case, 'championing an idea' is synonymous with one's desire to act morally. Secondly, an idea can serve as the *symbolic expression of the trends that characterise an era*. In this regard, an idea can be understood as the actual *zeitgeist* that prevails within society. Just as the idea of authority has been able

---

1   Author's Note (AN): Niekisch (Ernst), *Politik und Idee* [TN: Politics and Idea], Widerstands-Verlag, Dresden, 1929.

to dominate society at certain times, it is the idea of rebellion for rebellion's sake — of emancipation from authority — that characterises
ours, for instance. Here, the idea acts as a societal ideal in the most
common meaning of the word. Last but not least, there is also a third
meaning, one in which the term 'idea' designates one's *notion* of a
thing: one can have a certain idea of the State, of the nation, of the
economy, etc. As different as they might be, however, what these three
meanings of the word 'idea' have in common is that they all possess a
certain prescriptive value. Morality thus clearly indicates what should
be, whereas the ideals of an era take on the *form* of what must be.
Ideas, on the other hand, are understood as concepts and theories that
are to be implemented on a practical level. Since time immemorial,
man has sought to subordinate what *is* to what *should be*, which is why
moralists, clergymen, idealists and technocrats are all too tempted to
subject the 'art of possibilities', which politics undoubtedly is, to their
own rules.

And yet, politics remains an eternal sphere of disappointment to
them, as it never corresponds to their expectations. Abiding solely by
its own laws, politics stubbornly refuses to be ensnared in the web of
ideas. And it is from the fact that there is indeed a discrepancy between
ideas and politics, a heterogeneity of ends between morals, science and
politics, that *political realism* is born. Just as the purpose of economics
is not that of art, the aim of politics does not match that of morals.
Although the first distinction is obvious to everyone, the second, by
contrast, raises many questions and even horrifies. Such a fluster is
admittedly not difficult to understand. Since politics does not follow
the same rules as morality, it is perhaps no more than sheer opportun-
ism, pragmatism, an unbridled search for efficacy and mere power
worship, right? As we shall soon see, however, such an interpretation
is as unreasonable as it is excessive.

In no way does what is conveniently termed 'political realism' constitute a unified doctrine, nor is it a proper school of thought. It rather
refers to a sort of *habitus*, i.e. a mental predisposition, a study- or

research-related point of view that strives to clarify the rules which politics abides by.[1] In order to specify these rules, however, one must be able to phenomenologically analyse political life, independently of all that is essentially moral. The thinkers who do venture that far are naturally loathed, maligned and perceived as miserable cynics. It is of course Machiavelli that first springs to mind, as do for instance Thucydides,[2] Gabriel Naudé,[3] Thomas Hobbes, Vilfredo Pareto,[4] Max Weber, Betrand de Jouvenel,[5] Raymond Aron,[6] Carl Schmitt, Jules Monnerot[7] and Julien Freund,[8] who, despite their occasionally very different convictions, all share the characteristic of wanting to clarify the mechanisms inherent in politics.

As for the purpose of our current work, it is thus not that of introducing a political doctrine nor of dogmatically imposing a set of abstract principles meant to define politics once and for all, but rather

---

1   AN: Imatz (Arnaud), introduction to the work of Dalmacio Negro Pavón entitled *La Loi de fer de l'oligarchie — Pourquoi le gouvernement du peuple, par le peuple, pour le peuple est un leurre* [TN: The Iron Law of Oligarchy — Why the Rule of the People, by the People and for the People is a Delusion]. L'Artilleur, 2019.

2   Translator's Note (TN): An Athenian historian and general, Thucydides is considered by some to be the 'father of scientific history'. His History of the Peloponnesian War focuses on the fifth-century BC war between Sparta and Athens until the year 411 BC.

3   TN: Gabriel Naudé (2 February 1600–10 July 1653) was a French librarian and scholar who wrote a plethora of books on various topics.

4   TN: Born Wilfried Fritz Pareto, Vilfredo Federico Damaso Pareto was an Italian polymath who introduced the concept of Pareto efficiency and helped develop the field of microeconomics.

5   TN: Bertrand de Jouvenel des Ursins was a French philosopher, political economist, and futurist who taught at several prestigious universities.

6   TN: One of France's most famous thinkers, Raymond Claude Ferdinand Aron was a philosopher, sociologist, political scientist, historian, and journalist.

7   TN: Jules Monnerot was a French essayist and journalist.

8   TN: Labelled an 'unsatisfied liberal-conservative', Julien Freund (8 January 1921–10 September 1993) was a French philosopher and sociologist.

to present a certain perspective of the political that allows one to discern the issues that are specific to it. Such a clarification effort is indeed essential to evade the two main dangers resulting from the confusion between morality and politics: for politics to be absorbed by morals, thus becoming depoliticised, or worse still, for politics to use morals as a means to grant itself a clear conscience and enable itself to justify actions steeped in dishonesty, resentment or greed.

Faced with ideologists who announce the end or the withering of the political, what we have before us instead is the *autonomy* of the political. Not only can the political never be reduced to mere morality, economics or aesthetics, it is also not to be defined as trickery, as a superimposed element of human societies which one could readily do without. Not at all, for the political is an intrinsic component of any society, a fundamental fact in our human existence. If the political exists, it is first and foremost because man is a social and historical being that must organise a society whose very progression is not predestined to stop. Once kinship systems and tribal ties no longer suffice to resolve internal conflicts within the community, it is the political that emerges as an autonomous category, organising the society in question and setting common objectives.

However, just because politics is not an accidental result of convention, it does not mean that it represents an immovable and rigid notion. Although it is indeed a fundamental activity in our human existence, it is still required to take on a range of shapes in real life. And yet, as reminded by numerous philosophers from Plato to Vilfredo Pareto, change can only be understood in relation to what does not change; which is why one usually distinguishes *the political*, an essential category, from *politics*, which enables the former's specific and ever-changing implementation. As summarised by Julien Freund, however, 'although political revolutions do indeed exist, there is no such thing as a revolution in the political'.[9]

---

9   AN: Freund (Julien), *L'Essence du Politique* [TN: The Essence of the Political], Dalloz, 2004. P. IX.

We therefore have no intention at this point to study *politics* as a practical and contingent activity, but rather to present the conceptual framework of *the political*, within which the former unfolds. To this end, we shall highlight the primary intuitions that governed the drafting of the works of such great thinkers as Machiavelli, Hobbes and Carl Schmitt, so as to shed light upon the preconditions without which it becomes impossible to ponder the political.

CHAPTER I

MACHIAVELLI AND THE ART OF ACTION

A s SOON AS ONE tackles the topic of the relationship between law, morality and power, one single name emerges, towering above all others: Machiavelli's. It has now been five centuries that his name is adorned with a halo of genuine glory and there is an abundant literature that describes him as either a great thinker or a monster devoid of any and all sense of morality. His name having inspired the very coining of a particularly widespread adjective, one would be hard-pressed to find another political author that has exerted a comparable sort of influence. The reason behind this influence, however, is not immediately obvious, as Carl Schmitt himself points out:

> And yet, he was neither a great statesman nor a great theoretician. His political activity in the service of Florence remained without noteworthy repercussions within the issues that he himself dealt with on behalf of his native city in his role as president of the chancellery or as a member of several delegations to both France and Germany. Never did he find himself occupying a decisive or instrumental position. He did write a certain number of interesting reports, but was completely unable to impact the fact that Florence's foreign policy was, at the time, quite weak and deplorable. In his domestic policy positions, he was always most unfortunate. In 1513, the defeat of the Democrats, to whom he belonged, determined his own fate. The

victorious Medici party proceeded to imprison him, torture him, before ultimately releasing him, probably because he lacked political significance. He thus spent the remaining 14 years of his life exiled to the countryside, in a small house located along the road that led from Florence to Rome, surviving on the revenues generated by a small farm; in short, as a poor wretch who attempted to return to the political scene, but all in vain. Such was the situation in which the two works that would make him famous saw the light of day, namely *Discourses on the First Decade of Titus Livius* and *The Prince*, both of which would only be published after his death. Nothing about his life was brilliant or in any way grandiose or heroic.[1]

So, if his reputation does not stem from his actual life, he definitely owes it to his *Prince*, a work that has withstood the test of time. Even there, however, its longevity might be surprising. The wording of *The Prince* is admittedly very eloquent, displaying a classic sort of clarity and simplicity while being imbued with humanistic culture; and yet, it fails to offer readers as many prophetic and memorable flights as Nietzsche's writings, for instance. Nor does his work possess the loftiness of Plato's dialogues or the systematic expressiveness of Aristotle's books. In vain would one sift through it in search of a new theory of the State or of a historical philosophy worthy of Saint Augustine or Hegel.

Could it be, then, that his fame is due to his alleged 'immorality'? The latter, however, does seem quite unspectacular today when compared with the writings of Lenin and Trotsky. Neither was his work a radical novelty at the time. As pointed out by Max Weber, Hindu literature had already presented us with a classic form of radical 'Machiavellianism' (in the popular sense beastowed upon the

---

1   AN: Schmitt (Carl), Machiavelli — 'On the Occasion of 22 June 1927', Krisis, issue number 28, *Politics?*, 2006.

latter) through Kautilya's[2] *Arthashastra,* long before the Christian era. 'Compared to this document, Machiavelli's *Prince* is a harmless book.'[3]

If Machiavelli was indeed innovative and his work has actually impacted his readers to such an extent, it is not so much the result of his immorality as that of his perfect honesty. Had Machiavelli been truly 'Machiavellian', he would never have admitted, in a display of characteristic simplicity, that, in politics, it is always preferable to give the impression of being *pious* than to actually be so. He would rather have joined the choir-like throngs of flatterers praising the prince's righteousness. Driven by a sincere love of his country, which he wanted to 'rid of barbarians', he set out to describe without judgement in the same way one would pen the natural history of men, with the aim of carrying out specific actions without indulging in intellectual speculation. Such is the guiding principle of his entire work, which remains, even today, an essential reference.

It is customary to say that Machiavelli was a thinker of the Italian Renaissance, which is obviously correct from a chronological point of view, since Niccolo Machiavelli was born in 1469 in Florence and died in 1527. And yet, if the Renaissance is indeed characterised by a return to the thoughts and culture of antiquity, it is clear that Machiavelli stands out quite noticeably from the rest of his contemporaries. In point of fact, this return to antiquity was mainly achieved through the rediscovery of ancient philosophers such as Marsilio Ficino. And although Machiavelli did also undertake to return to antiquity, it was not in order to draw inspiration from the philosophies of Plato and Aristotle, which he was incidentally very familiar with, but rather to derive such inspiration from the historians of old, including Thucydides and Titus Livius. Machiavelli's secret consisted in taking specific examples from

---

2   TN: Kautilya, otherwise known as Chanakya, is said to have been a Brahmin who assisted the first Mauryan emperor Chandragupta in his rise to power and the establishment of the Maurya Empire.

3   AN: Weber (Max), *Scholarship and Politics in the Disenchanted World.* Paris, Union Générale d'Éditions, '10/18', 1963, p. 177.

the history of antiquity so as to develop a conception of politics that antiquity itself would have rejected.

At the time, philosophy was still largely dominated by Aristotelian principles, thus analysing human life in light of the notions of *good* and *ends*, hierarchised in accordance with their different levels. From this perspective, the end that the City strives for designates a higher and definitive sort of good. Indeed, in ancient and mediaeval philosophy, politics was inseparable from morality and even constituted one of its branches, with politics playing the same role for society as morality did for the individual. A legislator must, therefore, not only be virtuous, but also be able to guide his own citizens towards virtue by means of good laws.

And it is in this regard that Machiavelli radically breaks with philosophical tradition. Having had the opportunity to witness the fact that any form of political ideal often turns into a policy of the ideal, that is, into a demand for perfection so pure and absolute that it pushes one to espouse inaction, his ambition was not to establish an ideal philosophers' State, but to identify the objective laws that govern the rule of men, with the aim of achieving the greatest possible efficacy. Metaphysical abstractions must thus give way to experience and political regimes must be considered and evaluated from an experimental point of view. 'It appears to me more appropriate to follow up the effectual truth [*la verità effettuale*] of the matter than the imagination of it,' he writes. What constitutes the very object of his reflections is the specific political situation in hand and the most appropriate manner of dealing with it — which is why Machiavelli is less a Renaissance thinker than an 'untimely' one, as Nietzsche used to say: an untimely thinker whose thoughts, resulting from actual observation, seem valid for men at all times.

The Florentine is also untimely for the very strange reason that he comes across as a political theorist without an actual theory. This is in fact because Machiavelli was the very first to focus exclusively on political *action* itself, on its metamorphic dimension and its recurrent character, from which one is able to extract specific rules of action. In this respect, political action is defined by Machiavelli as an art, a technique that one can learn, practice, deepen, and teach. Strangely enough, however, men — including those most involved in the domain — have not until now, according to Machiavelli, paid much attention to the technique of this difficult art. They have always acted on instinct or feeling, according to their mood and their habits, sometimes behaving very correctly, but often very wrongly. Our statesmen, he says, are certainly in the habit of admiring the ancients and even of spending insane amounts of money on 'mere fragments of antique statue' that they are protective of, keeping them in their palaces, yet they do not take the time to pay attention to their own actions and study them. And yet, it is now high time that this happened and that we finally began to learn lessons from our history, says Machiavelli, instead of allowing it to unfold before us like a parade of motley figures. And it is for this very reason that his two major political works, namely *Discourses* and *The Prince*, comprise an entire array of political advice and recommendations, inspired and supported by examples taken from both ancient history and 15th-to 16th-century Italy. As can be read read in the introduction to the first book of his *Discourses*, Machiavelli is aware of his opening up 'a new path'. Unlike his predecessors, Machiavelli does not propose that his readers transpose an ideal into reality, but reveals a set of habits that one should familiarise themselves with and dissect. 'What is medicine if not the experience had by ancient doctors, (and) on which present doctors base their judgments?' he asks. Now, if the doctor bases his knowledge and practice on the experience accumulated by his predecessors, why should statesmen start with an abstract rule, a moral law established since the dawn of time? It is from the very effectiveness of history that one must draw the substance to perfect one's own art.

Machiavelli's work thus aims to uncover rules that lead to success in the political domain. The term 'rules', however, should not be taken too literally. A game of chess or checkers has, in the genuine sense, rules that no player can break. The 'rules' of political action, by contrast, are more loosely defined and therefore more dangerous. And yet, there are certainly analogies between a game of chess and one's political actions. Just like a skilled chess player, a statesman can triumph using his solid understanding of all possible combinations and through his ability to adapt to the concrete configuration that he is presented with; but while, in any game of chess, the luck factor is reduced to a minimum, it is unthinkable to exclude it from every political game. Whereas the chessboard is a finite space, offering players the opportunity to take in all the elements of the game and develop a strategy with full knowledge of the facts, a political game does not have the same limitations. Indeed, some indeterminacy lies behind every decision or action, as a new element can always surface where one hardly expects it. And this is why, as Machiavelli acknowledges in chapter XXV of *The Prince*, it might well be the case that *fortune* decides half of our actions, leaving us with only one other half, or almost.[4]

In no way does this, however, constitute a serious objection to the attempt to pen a rulebook for political action, as we still have to keep a watchful eye over the second half that is allotted to us! Historical experience, condensed into rules (however imperfect these may be), thus allows the statesman to avoid having to fumble around in total darkness. Nevertheless, the mere idea that such rules can be drawn from history requires a prerequisite, namely that human nature remains unchanged throughout the centuries, at least in its essential features, so that the situations generated by history remain comparable. Indeed, if the knight or the bishop could suddenly follow a different movement on the chessboard, no rules could ever be established for their use. Machiavelli, however, is well aware of this necessary condition: 'as though heaven, the sun, the elements, and men had changed the order

---

4   AN: On this topic, one should refer to Jules Monnerot's *Laws of the Tragic*, in which the author develops the notion of *heterotelia* and reminds us that every action undertaken in this world leads to consequences that the agent could never have suspected.

of their motions and power, and were different from what they were in ancient times'! he says in response to the objection that any knowledge of the ancients would thus be useless. And he expressly repeats in several passages that it is only because men are always moved by the same passions that it is possible to predict the future, apply historical experience, and be involved in political science.[5]

> Anyone comparing the present with the past will soon perceive that in all cities and in all nations there prevail the same desires and passions as always have prevailed; for which reason it should be an easy matter for him who carefully examines past events, to foresee those which are about to happen in any republic, and to apply such remedies as the ancients have used in like cases; or finding none which have been used by them, to strike out new ones, such as they might have used in similar circumstances. But these lessons being neglected or not understood by readers, or, if understood by them, being unknown to rulers, it follows that the same disorders are common to all times.[6]

This persistence of human passions and drives through the ages does not, of course, prevent Machiavelli from discerning the profound changes that can affect human nature. He knows that there are times and peoples wherein virtue is widespread, piety authentic and love of one's country self-evident, and others in which these forces and structures have been completely and irremediably devoured by corruption. Education can render a man virile and uncompromising, but

---

5   AN: 'Is it not remarkable,' asks Julien Freund, 'that we still find ourselves fascinated by the history of the Peloponnesian War recounted by Thucydides or by the accounts of Alexander the Great's conquests, and above all, that we can find there ample material for our reflections on politics? If politics had become different over the centuries, if it had substantially changed under the effect of historical transformations and the becoming of civilisation, we would have great difficulty in understanding these events, as they would seem strange to us rather than anachronistic.' Freund (Julien), *L'Essence du politique*, Dalloz, 2004, p. 91.)

6   AN: Machiavelli, *Discourses on the First Decade of Titus Livius*, Book I, chapter XXXIX.

it can also soften and weaken him. Religion can lead men to grandiose actions, yet it can also make them so humble that they come to despise the world and stifle their natural desire to elevate themselves. This is, incidentally, the reproach that he targets Christianity with (see *Discourses II*, 2).

What does not change, however, is the presence of evil in the hearts of men. Observation is what leads him to state that the latter 'are ungrateful, voluble, dissemblers, anxious to avoid danger, and covetous of gain' (*The Prince*, XVII). And if all men are not intrinsically evil, in politics, one must suppose from the very outset that evil is inherent in the human species and that it is always capable of the worst deeds. And yet, once again, this is not a dogma — akin to that of original sin — that Machiavelli would strive to impose because of a certain metaphysical vision. Rather, it is a lesson that history would have us learn, namely that men are neither entirely good nor entirely evil, and that we must therefore expect the worst to avoid being toppled by a stroke of misfortune. We can therefore see it as a methodological precaution, as Fichte himself had very well acknowledged:[7]

> The fundamental principle of Machiavellian philosophy, and which — one adds without shame — is also ours, and acts, in our opinion, as the principle of any coherent theory of the State, is to be found in the following words by Machiavelli: "It is necessary to whoever disposes a republic and orders laws in it to presuppose that all men are bad, and that they always have to use the malignity of their spirit whenever they have a free opportunity for it."

Instead of waiting forever for men to finally become virtuous and brave enough to fight, or for an ideal set-up to come about for the sake of the country, Machiavelli suggests starting from the genuine and specific functioning of human societies and considering a plan of action based on men as they truly are. Whereas religion and moral philosophy espouse the moral duty to elevate men towards Good and

---

7   AN: Fichte (Johann Gottlieb), *Machiavelli and Other Philosophical and Political Writings of 1806–1807*, Paris, Payot, 1981, p. 55–56.

Virtue, politics, for its part, is not dedicated to transforming them. Its only option is to accept them as they are. Far from deploring this state of affairs or striving in vain to change it, one must instead attempt to come to terms with this evil. The vices of men are not necessarily obstacles to politics, as was once generally believed; they can even act as levers to more effectively achieve the set goal.

And this is where one faces the issue of 'Machiavellianism' as such, namely the precept attributed to Machiavelli, according to which 'the end justifies the means'. Indeed, there is a certain degree of confusion here. When Machiavelli ponders the technically sound means that allow one to respond to a given situation (pacifying a city, asserting one's power, killing a tyrant, foiling a plot, etc.), he follows a purely positive line of thought. 'He does not wonder about the meaning or merit of the goals that political actors set themselves, nor about their value and position in a hierarchy,'[8] notes Hans Freyer. The question of what is to be desired is completely absent from his theoretical reflections.[9] The mere fact that one seeks to achieve a goal is enough to arouse Machiavelli's interest, who merely analyses how best to achieve such a purpose. He does not decide whether to assassinate tyrants or unmask conspirators. He only examines the methods that enable one to achieve both aims, should one wish to do so. He does not long for Cesare Borgia or any other prince to claim the throne, but merely ponders the approach that they should adopt when in power. If he takes the trouble to equally examine both the virtuous actions and the crimes of the prince, it is not because he considers the latter to be more useful, but rather because they are frequent. In this sense, summarises

8   AN: Freyer (Hans), *Machiavelli*, VCH, Acta Humaniora, 1986, p. 53.

9   AN: Even if the question of the actual correctness of the desired purpose is excluded from Machiavelli's purely phenomenological and descriptive approach to power, this does not mean that he himself considered all political ends acceptable. On the contrary, he regularly cast blame, for example, on those who would divide Italy, while praising those who would unify it, although both goals were actually pursued and one could thus determine with equal precision how to achieve each.

Freyer, Machiavelli's doctrine is, first and foremost, a true technique of political action, carried out in full knowledge of the facts. The rules which it sets are, in their pure form, 'hypothetical imperatives', as they specify what must be done should ambition A, B or C be genuinely desired. *If one longs to achieve a certain end, one must consent to the necessary means.*

Now this Machiavellian question of means allows us to approach the essence of politics and clearly see, for the first time, what distinguishes it from other areas of human activity such as morality, aesthetics, or economics. Only the art of war, to which Machiavelli also devoted a treatise, is equal to politics in this regard since it is ultimately but a continuation of the latter using other means. In all other spheres of activity, the choice of means is restricted by general norms or long-standing customs. There is indeed such a thing as the 'rules of the game', either in the literal or figurative sense, regardless of whether they are determined by explicit or tacit agreement, criminal law, moral law, or any other norm system. 'If a chess player were to shoot his opponent's queen with his revolver', compares Hans Freyer, 'he would immediately be disqualified, and his victory would not be considered a triumph.' In politics, however, there is no such thing, says Machiavelli. On the contrary, victory is always considered a victory, since there is no referee to disqualify the victor after the fact, nor is there any criminal judge to condemn him. And yet, the whole scandal surrounding Machiavelli's work stems from this, as it brings a secret out into the open, namely the tacit agreement between all participants that all means are indeed acceptable. For politics is not a game, but an absolute struggle.

And if politics is defined as an absolute struggle, the prerequisite of any political theory must therefore be to teach people the technicalities involved in it. Machiavelli's novelty does not consist so much in presenting a new political theory and breaking with the one that characterised classical political philosophy,[10] but in one's awareness of the ever-changing, dangerous and *risky* reality on which all political action is based.

> [M]any have imagined republics and principalities for themselves which have never been seen or known to exist in reality, for the distance is so great between how we live and how we ought to live that he who abandons what is done for what ought to be done learns his ruin rather than his preservation. (*The Prince*, XV)

Now, if the struggle is indeed absolute, it is in this respect that it remains completely unbridled in one's choice of means, yet the description of the latter is in no way an (im)moral suggestion as such. For a lie is still a lie and murder still murder, as constantly and explicitly emphasised by Machiavelli himself. 'When it comes to technical observations, however, there are no values of substance, only ones of function, and there is no good and evil, only adequate and inadequate means.'[11]

> [I]t is found in ordinary affairs that one never seeks to avoid one trouble without running into another; but prudence consists in knowing how to distinguish the character of troubles, and for choice to take the lesser evil. (*The Prince*, chapter XXI)

---

10 AN: Since the days of Aristotle, classical philosophy had always differentiated between six forms of political regime, three being good and virtuous and three negative and corrupt: monarchy and tyranny, aristocracy and oligarchy, the republic and democracy.

11 Freyer (Hans), op. cit., p. 57.

CHAPTER II

THOMAS HOBBES AND OBEDIENCE

T HE TECHNICALITY OF the action is not, however, everything. For if the reality on which political action is based is indeed changeable and risky, as demonstrated by Machiavelli, it thus requires a foundation that grants it long-term value. And yet, as correctly highlighted by Pierre Manent,[1] 'one cannot deduce the legitimacy, appropriateness or even mere necessity of one institution or another from Machiavelli's writings. One may even wonder whether there is room for any institution in the world as he himself describes it, a world based on the fertility of violent initiative and on actions that are an appropriate source of fear. I would say that every institution presupposes a certain kind of positivity, a fair amount of harmony and consistency within the political body, one that seems foreign to Machiavelli.'[2] Remedying this deficiency will ultimately be both the task and the accomplishment of Thomas Hobbes.

The fundamental issue pervading Hobbesian thought is, in fact, that of obedience: Why is there authority and obedience, and why do

---

1   TN: Pierre Manent is a French political scientist and academic who teaches political philosophy.

2   AN: Manent (Pierre), *Histoire intellectuelle du libéralisme* [TN:The Intellectual History of Liberalism], Paris, Calmann-Lévy, 1987, p. 51.

we find them in all political societies? Where does the colossal power that some men hold over millions of others truly come from? Indeed, it was La Bruyère[3] who asked:

> If you were told that all the cats in a vast country had gathered together in their thousands on a plain, and after having mewed for all they were worth had rushed at one another furiously, lashing out with tooth and claw; that this affray had left nine or ten thousand cats lying on the field of battle, so that the air for ten leagues around reeked of their stench, wouldn't you say: "*That's the most appalling pandemonium ever heard of!*"[4]

And yet, as soon as a sovereign declares war on another, all his men line up in battle array without questioning this decision. How can one account for the fact that men would agree to obey one of their own in such a manner?

In some way, this issue has always arisen in practice, i.e. in real political life, yet it never arose, from a theoretical perspective, in the classical, Greek or mediaeval formulation of the political problem. However, the questions that Aristotle asks in his *Politics* are rather the following: what is the best political regime? And who is most apt to command others — the people, the wise, the rich or the aristocrats? Now, the question of *who* should command is, of course, not the same as wondering *why* one is to obey, even if the two questions are clearly connected. It is therefore a new question in the history of ideas, or, alternatively, what *is* new is, at the very least, the intensity with which Hobbes asks it.

In ancient times, the answer would have been that political power stems either from nature or from God. Ever since Europe entered the modern era, however, neither of these two explanations seems satisfactory any more: the power that a man exercises over other men comes from men themselves, says Thomas Hobbes, who is among those

---

3   TN : Famous for his satire, Jean de La Bruyère (16 August 1645–11 May 1696) was a French philosopher and moralist.

4   AN: La Bruyère (Jean de), *Les Caractères* [TN: The Characters], chapter XII, 'Of Opinions'.

authors 'that have placed particular emphasis on the impenetrable, arbitrary and troubling essence of both command and obedience.'[5] The ethical humanitarianism that dominates modern democratic societies may well discredit the notions of command and obedience, as well as the obscure irrationality that underlies them, but it will never manage to purge them completely. This is because, 'from the point of view of the very essence of the political,' says Freund, 'the obscure forces that drive both command and obedience have at least as much importance, and sometimes even more so, than the research carried out into the disparity of power and institutions from one society to another and from one era to the next.'

The contribution made by Hobbesian thought is not a question of exalting or denigrating the virtues of command and obedience, but one of acknowledging things as they truly are. What emphasising this dialectic of command and obedience actually implies is not that one is to submit to one form of power or another, but that one must recognise it to be the foundation of the political and to acknowledge the fact that it determines all political order. 'It is not a matter of yielding to the arguments and wishes of justification, as a foundation need not be justified. Otherwise, it would cease to be a foundation.'[6] It is only by obeying another man that men bestow power upon the latter. If they no longer choose to obey him, the power in question vanishes. And that is why command and obedience give rise to the political. Objecting to this fact would be a most futile endeavour.

It is thus probably no coincidence that the relationship between politics and obedience was given so much significance in the 17th century, especially by Thomas Hobbes, but also by Spinoza and Locke, among others. Just as Machiavellian thought was due to the fragmentation experienced by the Italy of the Renaissance, the perceptiveness of the above-mentioned authors undoubtedly stemmed from the weakening of their respective states in the aftermath of the wars of

---

5 AN: Freund (Julien), *The Essence of the Political*, p. 103.

6 AN: *Ibid.*, p. 105.

religion. Having watched the Catholic and Protestant parties wage a bloody civil war against one another throughout Europe, with each of them convinced of their own acting in the name of religious morality and superior ethical principles, the authors of this century came to the conclusion that morality could never replace politics. Directing political action to serve morality or religion leads to robbing one's enemy of all legitimacy and sparking civil war in one's own country as soon as people can no longer agree on the same conception of morality. It would therefore be better, they said, to re-establish politics in its own rights by limiting it to strictly political ends, that is to say, to the preservation of domestic order and to the latter's protection against external threats. This, however, is only possible through obedience.

To determine these strictly political ends, Hobbes conducted a thought experiment by imagining a 'state of nature' for men prior to their entering political and social life. Before Rousseau, Hobbes thus reveals himself to be one of the first thinkers of the *Social Contract*. It is not a matter of stressing the limits and narrowness of 'contractualist' thinking, as Joseph de Maistre clearly highlighted.[7] What must be kept in mind is that in Hobbes' case, this reasoning aspires to *geometric* and not historical validity. The social contract has no empirical or historical reality; it is founded solely on reason.

What is this state of nature like, then, according to Hobbes? He writes:

---

7   AN: 'If man has indeed moved on from a state of nature, in the vulgar sense of the word, to a state of civilisation, either by means of a common agreement or *by chance* (I still speak the language of the insane), why have nations not had as much spirit or as much happiness as individuals have, and how have they never agreed on a global society to end the quarrels of nations, just as they have agreed on national sovereignty to end that of individuals?' Maistre (Joseph de), *Les Soirées de Saint-Pétersbourg* [TN: St Petersburg Dialogues], Paris, Garnier frères, p. 12.

> The condition of men outside civil society (the condition one may call the state of nature) is no other than a war of all men against all men [*bellum omnium contra omnes*]; and in that war all men have a right to all things.

Left to themselves, in their 'natural' and wild state, men can only kill each other. Without the discipline that makes them fit for political society, men are like capricious infants:

> Unless you give children all they ask for, they are peevish, and cry, aye and strike their parents sometimes, and all this they have from nature, yet are they free from guilt, neither may we properly call them wicked; first, because they cannot hurt; next, because wanting the free use of reason they are exempted from all duty. These when they come to riper years, having acquired power whereby they may do hurt, if they shall continue to do the same things, then truly they both begin to be, and are properly accounted wicked.[8]

However, he goes on to add, a wicked man is no different from a robust child or a man who has the soul of a child; that is to say, the wickedness that governs the "natural" state is nothing but a lack of reason and discipline. Just as the child shrieks and hits others when he/she does not get exactly what he/she wants, natural man considers himself to have a right to everything, a *jus in omnia*. Due to this very fact, it is fear that dwells in the hearts of all these men. And, as correctly pointed out by Hobbes, the cause of this mutual fear depends on 'the natural equality of all men':

> For if we look on men full-grown, and consider how brittle the frame of our human body is, (which perishing, all its strength, vigour, and wisdom itself perisheth with it) and how easy a matter it is, even for the weakest man to kill the strongest, there is no reason why any man trusting to his own strength should conceive himself made by nature above others: they are equals who can do equal things one against the other; but they who can do the greatest things, (namely, kill) can do equal things. All men therefore

---

8   AN: 19. Hobbes (Thomas), *On the Citizen*, translated by S. Sorbière, Paris, GF Flammarion, 1987, p. 73.

among themselves are by nature equal; the inequality we now discern, hath its spring from the civil law.[9]

If men, therefore, agree to surrender a part of their freedom to obey power, it is because they require protection. In 'natural' equality, however, no one can protect us. And that is why, demonstrates Hobbes, the connection between protection and obedience is the only explanation for the origin of power: he who does not have the power to protect others does not have the right to ask them to obey, either. And conversely: he who seeks protection and accepts it does not have the right to withdraw obedience. Hobbes thus structures his reasoning as follows: from weakness stems danger, from danger fear, from fear the need for security, and from this the need for a protective apparatus with a more or less complex organisation. He does remind us, however, that despite all the protective measures, any man can kill another at the right time. Even the weakest man can find himself in a position to overthrow the strongest and most powerful one. In this respect, men are truly equal, insofar as they are all threatened with imminent death.

Perceiving the absurdity and evil of this state of nature, human reason thus seeks appropriate means of peace. And that is how a new form of art is born, one that displays a new purpose: politics. Every person must therefore commit themselves to give up their unlimited rights. Without the presence of a sword, covenants are but words.[10] The only guarantee that every man's right will indeed be respected thus lies in the threat of punishment. Every person renounces their absolute right over things in order to transfer it all to the one to whom they entrust sovereignty, i.e. to the Leviathan, the 'artificial man' or 'mortal God', under the condition that the latter maintains civil peace, using force if necessary. And that is precisely how man is as much a wolf to man — *homo homini lupus* — as a god to man — *homo homini deus*.

9 AN: *Ibid.*, p. 95.

10 AN: 'Covenants without the sword are but words', *Leviathan*, chapter CXVIII.

Of course, the aim here is not that of highlighting all the ideas and theories comprised in *Leviathan*, a 'must-read book that one could spend a lifetime commenting on', to use Diderot's words. Nor is it up to us to pronounce ourselves on the legacy of Hobbes' work or on the place that it occupies in the history of ideas. If Thomas Hobbes interests us here, as we reflect on political realism, it is because the author was one of the first to expose the dialectic of obedience and protection in such a radical manner.[11] The very mission entrusted to power is that of maintaining social cohesion and peace within the community. By definition, however, it can only fulfil this role if it is powerful enough; indeed, any decline in power automatically leads to a waning in authority and therefore to disorder and chaos. To adopt the language of Thomas Hobbes himself, a weakening of power causes society to plunge, once again, into a 'state of nature', i.e. into civil war. As can be well understood, therefore, the function of the theory of man's state of nature is to demonstrate that sovereign might and its power of protection are a presupposition of politics. Protection (or security, Spinoza would state) is thus the essential reason for one's obedience. Consequently, however, as soon as power ceases to guarantee such protection, obedience vanishes as well.

Although Hobbes thus recognises the great significance of action and political art, just as Machiavelli did, he bestows upon them a more lasting purpose than the mere conservation of power. The sovereign institutes and guarantees, through the laws that he enacts, the protection of his people, and his legitimacy does not stem from his wisdom or virtue, but from his strength and ability to ensure this protection.

---

11 AN: '*Protego ergo obligo* — such is the *cogito ergo sum* of the State, and a theory of the State that does not systematically take this dictum into account will never be more than a fragmentary and flawed sketch. Hobbes declared that he had written his *Leviathan* with the intention of making once again apparent to men *the mutual relation between Protection and Obedience*, which both human nature and divine right force us to respect in absolute terms.' Schmitt (Carl), *The Notion of the Political*, translated by M.-L. Steinhauser, Paris, Flammarion, Champs classiques Collection, p. 94.

'It's not wisdom, but authority that makes a law', declares the English philosopher. And yet, sovereign authority entails a genuine paradox: for it is rooted in decision, that is to say, in an arbitrary and discretionary will, and it is precisely as such that it acts as a guarantee against randomness and disorder. And it is this very *decision-making* which, with all the authority that it bears, fights against the irrationality of multiple, equal yet dispersed wills by introducing hierarchy through discipline, much more so than any rational and abstract theories ever could.

Through these two notions of obedience and command, revealed to us by Hobbes and later developed in all their scope by Julien Freund, we therefore reach into the very heart of the political issue. Raymond Aron summed it up very correctly when he stated:

> To me, the constant problematic of the political sphere does not seem that hard to define. Ultimately, the issue that we have always raised under the notion of *political problem* is that of simultaneously justifying authority and obedience. [...] Is it possible to justify both obedience and the refusal to obey? Can one validate both authority and the limits of this authority? This is the eternal issue characterising the political domain, in which all regimes, taken as they are, only serve as flawed solutions.[12]

The real issue is thus not to put an end to the relationship between command and obedience or to weaken it, as put forth by anarchist theories, for instance, because it is futile for one to hope for any kind of policy without this relationship. As Julien Freund highlights, it is rather a question of establishing, on a practical level, the 'right' dialectic between these two notions; hence the importance, for any philosophy or political theory, of being aware of this rationale.

> Hereby it is manifest that during the time men live without a common power to keep them all in awe, they are in that condition which is called war; and such a war as is of every man against every man (*Leviathan*, chapter XIII).

---

12 AN: Aron (Raymond), *The Sociology of Industrial Societies — Outline of a Theory of Political Regimes*, 1961.

CHAPTER III

CARL SCHMITT AND THE AUTONOMY OF THE POLITICAL

AFTER MACHIAVELLI and Hobbes, let us move forward across the centuries to look at one of their distant successors, Carl Schmitt, who would explicitly lay claim to this lineage by naming his house in Plettenberg *San Casciano*, in reference to the exiled Florentine's place of residence. Similarly, Hobbes would always occupy, just like Donoso Cortés, an important place in both Schmitt's thinking and in the development of his *decisionism*.[1] And even though Schmitt would later become more critical of the English philosopher,[2] he would nonetheless declare in 1954 that Thomas Hobbes was and remained 'the most modern philosopher to ponder the purely human

---

1 AN: Having explained the historical circumstances in which Donoso Cortés glorified dictatorship, Schmitt notes: 'Such is the result that Hobbes also arrived at, by virtue of the same logic of decisionist thought, even if it was indeed mixed with mathematical relativism. *Auctoritas non veritas facit legem*' (*Political Theology*, published in 1988 by Gallimard, Paris, pages 60–61).

2 AN: Particularly after reading the *Commentary* that Leo Strauss wrote on his *Notion of Politics*, demonstrating that there was, according to him, a contrast between Hobbes as the founder of liberalism and Carl Schmitt as its critic.

aspect of power'.[3] What Carl Schmitt adopts above all from these two thinkers is the notion that war, and not peace, constitutes the horizon of politics. The essential movement of modernity, however, of which liberalism is the driving force, is, according to him, characterised by the negation of this polemical horizon, and therefore by the negation of politics. For liberalism has distorted all political notions and given them a new face, in order to obscure this primary relationship of conflict. He goes on to add that 'in liberal thought, the political concept of struggle is thus transformed into competition from an economic perspective, and into debate from a mental angle,' and war and peace, defined as two clearly distinct states, 'are replaced by the dynamics of perpetual competition and endless debate'. 'The State becomes Society and the latter, seen from the perspective of both ethics and the mind, becomes an image of Humanity.'[4]

The liberal bourgeois, however, are not alone in this endeavour, for they are joined on this level by socialist and Marxist ideologists. Some long to do away with politics by means of legal imperialism, in an effort to guarantee their bourgeois security, while others resort to ideological supremacy instead. As early as 1923, Schmitt had already noted this fact in his *Political Theology*:

> Nothing is more modern today than the struggle against politics. American financiers, industrial technicians, Marxist socialists and revolutionary anarcho-syndicalists are joining forces in embracing the slogan according to which the non-objective prevalence of politics over the objectivity of economic life must be eliminated. Only technical, organisational, economic, and sociological tasks are to subsist, with political issues expected to disappear. Furthermore, the type of economic and technical thinking that dominates today's world is incapable of discerning a political idea. The modern State seems to have truly become what Max Weber saw in it: a large corporation.

---

3   AN: Schmitt (Carl), *Gespräch über die Macht und den Zugang zum Machthaber* [TN: Conversation on Power and Access to the Ruler], Klett-Cotta, 2008, p. 18.

4   AN: Schmitt (Carl), *The Concept of the Political, op. cit.*, p. 117.

The proponents of these different modern ideologies are, of course, unable to escape politics and attempt therefore to practice it by speaking an *anti-political* sort of language, thus blurring people's clear understanding of the impasses that they come up against. To Schmitt, it is consequently a matter of recapturing the 'truth' of the political by providing us with a 'theoretical framework' for the very issue of the political. Through his *Notion of Politics*, Julien Freund tells us, his objective is to determine the criterion, that is to say the sign that allows one to recognise whether a problem is a political one or not, and to discern, therefore, what is purely political, independently of any other relationship. Carl Schmitt's goal is thus absolutely not that of offering us an ideal political theory, as Plato did in his *Republic* and Maurras in *Inquiry into the Monarchy*, for instance, but rather that of raising the issue of what is exclusively political and not legal, moral, statal or economic. Where Machiavelli had fully focused on political action itself, highlighting its ever-changing and risky nature, Schmitt seeks to provide us with a theoretical framework.

But why is it important to outline and define this theoretical framework? For the very good reason that, when talking about politics or political theory, one often runs the risk of raising mere historical manifestations linked to a specific period to the level of the very essence of the political.

As Schmitt points out, the field of politics undergoes constant changes in accordance with the specific nature of the forces present. He then gives us an example of what constitutes a mistake: while studying the Greek *polis*, Aristotle arrived at certain definitions of the political, definitions that were then adopted by the scholars of the Middle Ages, although they themselves were aiming for something completely different. Aristotle's concern was to provide a definition of what a just city was, in harmony with the model of the Greek city-state, whereas mediaeval people were focused on the opposition between spiritual power and worldly or temporal power, a notion that was utterly foreign to Aristotle.

Schmitt, however, highlights a similar mistake that was increasingly common in his time (and which remains very widespread today), which consists in amalgamating *politics* and *state*, i.e. in defining politics through the state and all that relates to it. The adjective *political* is generally assimilated, in one way or another, to the concept of the *statal* or, at the very least, put in relation with the notion of state. Similarly, the state itself is often defined as a political entity, which results in a vicious circle where each of these two notions accounts for the other.

This confusion dates back to the 16th century, when the religious unity of Europe was shattered by the Wars of Religion between Catholics and Protestants. Scholars that were referred to as 'politicians' in France, including Jean Bodin, for instance, took up the cause of the state as a superior and neutral unit, beyond any and all religious parties. And it was this tendency that prevailed in the re-defining of Europe after the Wars of Religion, around the 16th and 17th centuries, and what has come to be known as the Treaty of Westphalia. In order to pacify the continent, the sovereign state then became the model of political unity par excellence. As for Schmitt, he was a great admirer of this Westphalian order, of this *jus gentium europaeum* whose ultimate guarantor he considered himself to be. The state, this 'masterpiece of the European condition and Western rationality', as Schmitt put it, found itself holding the total monopoly of political decision-making during this period. Now, it was at this time that all the classical concepts of political theory were formulated (not only Thomas Hobbes, but also Alberico Gentili, Grotius, Pufendorf and Rousseau, for example). Back then, identifying politics with what was statal was essentially justified. Indeed, the classical European state had succeeded in a quite astonishing feat, namely of establishing peace within its borders and excluding hostility as a legal concept. 'Private war', which was recognised by mediaeval law, ceased to exist, and the State had managed to pacify religious denominations. What reigned within the borders, says Schmitt, was the police (following the motto 'tranquillity, security and order'), and only the foreign policy practiced by a sovereign state towards other sovereign states was regarded as truly political, in particular when it came to deciding on their mutual relations of friendship, hostility or neutrality. Three centuries after this Westphalian order, however, says Schmitt, 'the era of the state is experiencing a decline'. And yet, this decline is paradoxical in that the modern state is increasingly degenerating into what he terms a *total state*.[5] And this is why it is important to separate or, at least, conceptually distinguish the notions of state and politics, which are no longer one and the same. Hence the first sentence of his text: 'The concept of the state presupposes that of politics.' What is meant by this is that not only can there be political activity outside the statal framework, but politics would continue even if the state itself were to disappear. As long as man lives in society, politics will simply remain an indispensable activity, since all social life must be organized. On the other hand, the state is merely the modern way of perceiving this organisation; it is but a type of political organisation that could potentially be replaced by another over the course of our historical development. Consequently, it is impossible to imagine a society that would not be politically organised, yet it is possible to conceive of this organisation within a framework that is not that of the state. There can be politics without a state, but there can be no state without politics. In summary, therefore, Carl Schmitt does not believe in the disappearance of the political genre, as it can be involved in any type of activity due to the fact that it constitutes a notion that relates to collective anthropology. In this respect, as pointed out by Julien Freund, political activity can be described as *substance*. The State, by

---

5   AN: The concept of the total state is a complex notion in Carl Schmitt's thought, but one can try to summarise it in a few words: the total state is a state that is no longer centred solely around its sovereign and political aspects and one that is increasingly characterised by its interventionism within society, which blurs all the old dividing lines that separate heterogeneous spheres (the religious from the secular, politics from economics, the state from civil society, etc.). As a result, politics as such increasingly evades the grasp of the state, thus spreading to all layers of society.

contrast, can be described as a *body*, that is to say, a contingent form of sovereignty that can disappear or become depoliticised, without the political ever disappearing as a substance.

So, what is the famous criterion that allows one to distinguish the political? This is where the well-known antinomy between friend and foe emerges. Indeed, Carl Schmitt's approach consists in analysing the political phenomenon independently of any moral preconceptions, since morals and politics belong to distinct domains. Just like Machiavelli and Hobbes, he relinquishes all righteous sentiments and, instead, seeks criteria that are specific to the political domain and independent of the moral, aesthetic and economic spheres. Indeed, each of these domains, says Schmitt, possesses its own distinctions that are relatively autonomous. The fundamental distinctions are that of good and evil in the moral domain, the beautiful and the hideous in the aesthetical field and the useful and the harmful (or the profitable and the unprofitable) in the economic sphere. The question thus arises as to whether there is also a simple criterion for politics that would be of the same nature, analogous to the previous ones, without actually depending on them — an autonomous and, therefore, self-evident distinction. Schmitt's answer is the following: the specific distinction that characterises politics and to which all political acts and motives can be reduced is the well-known differentiation between friend and foe. This is indeed an autonomous distinction, as it could never be reduced to the other distinctions mentioned above. Just as what is good in the moral domain is not necessarily beautiful in the aesthetic field, nor profitable in the economic sphere, one's political foe is not necessarily bad in the moral sense nor aesthetically ugly. Nor will he necessarily play the role of an economic competitor; should it be advantageous, one could even do business with him. Of course, it is often the case that, psychologically speaking, our foe is treated as if he were bad or hideous, for the simple reason that the state or the body responsible for identifying the foe can draw on all the other exploitable distinctions to more readily achieve its ends. This fact, however, does not impact the autonomy of this type of differentiation, as what is morally condemnable or economically harmful does not necessarily make one a political enemy. The fact that a distinction which is as specific as the friend/foe discrimination can be isolated from other distinctions and understood as an autonomous element demonstrates in itself both the objective nature and the intrinsic autonomy of politics. These notions of friend and foe, however, must be taken in their specific and literal meaning and not as a metaphor or a symbol. The concept of an enemy implies the possibility of a struggle, a struggle that is not to be understood as mere competition, nor as a purely intellectual struggle as part of a discussion.

'The concepts of friend and foe, of combat,' says Schmitt, 'derive their objective meaning from their permanent relation to a very real fact, namely the possibility of causing the physical death of a man. War is born of hostility, and hostility signifies the existential negation of another being. War is but the ultimate actualisation of hostility.'[6] This does not imply that it is usual or normal, nor does it mean that it is perceived as ideal or desirable. It must necessarily, however, remain present in the form of a real possibility if the notion of enemy is to have any meaning whatsoever.

Political activity is thus defined by Schmitt as the product of a polarisation around a relationship of hostility and the possibility of war. However, this definition of politics should not be understood as being belligerent or militaristic — nor pacifistic, for that matter. A politically sound decision could, in fact, be that of avoiding war. War is neither the goal nor the end of politics; what it is instead is the hypothesis, the potential reality that governs, in its own way, the thoughts and actions of politicians. Anyone who thinks *politically* cannot act as if enemies did not exist. By means of an involuntary homage of vice to virtue, humanitarian, egalitarian and cosmopolitan theories themselves are very much political ones in the sense that they always give themselves

---

6   AN: Schmitt (Carl), *The Concept of the Political, op. cit.*, p. 71.

an enemy, an enemy who, in one way or another, constitutes the final obstacle before establishing a promised new order. Julien Freund remarks:

> From this point of view, Marxism indirectly confirms the correlation between enemy and politics, since in its opinion, the suppression of the latter depends on the annihilation of the former.[7]

Furthermore, one must not understand these notions of enemy and struggle in the narrow and limiting sense of an antagonism between two historically determined groups, as the Marxists do:

> *The history of all hitherto existing society is the history of class struggles.*[8]

Although Marx and Engels were right to grant this struggle such a central place in the history of men, they unilaterally and without justification restricted it to a class struggle.

As Julien Freund maliciously points out, the Greeks could have stated with equal accuracy that history was no more than the struggle between independent cities. Ludwig Gumplowicz's position is more correct, since he perceived politics as a ceaseless struggle between different communities whose purpose it is to establish one group's domination over the other.[9] Class struggle, however important it may be, is only one aspect of political struggle and its intensity varies according to the period in question, whereas political struggle in the broad sense is multifaceted and cannot be reduced to a single, specific type of conflict.

---

7   AN: Freund (Julien), *The Essence of the Political, op. cit.*, p. 444.

8   AN: Marx (Karl) and Engels (Friedrich), *The Communist Manifesto*, Paris, Librio, 2017, p. 29.

9   AN: 'It follows that the tendency of a social group to ensure the preservation and elevation of its own well-being becomes a tendency to dominate and enslave other social groups — hence the tendency to power, which must in turn be transformed into a struggle for domination over other social groups as soon as several groups with the same tendency meet.' (Gumplowicz [Ludwig], *Sociology and Politics*, Paris, V. Giard & E. Brière, 1898, p. 158).

Any genuine political unit must therefore acknowledge the possibility of conflict in advance and thus also the existence of other political units. As a result, the world is not a political unit, a *universum*, but rather a political *pluriversum*. This is precisely why the concept of a world state is an intellectual absurdity, but it is also the reason why there is no worse form of deception than waging war in the name of humanity. When a given state fights its political enemy in the name of humanity, it is not humanity's war, but that of a particular state which arrogates to itself a universal concept in order to identify with it at the expense of its adversary. Since the enemies of those that defend humanity are in fact outside humanity, there are no holds barred. As part of a realistic conception of politics, however, your enemy is not an eternal and diabolical figure, since those who are your foe one day could become a friend the next. Your enemy is thus not an entity to be abolished, like the bourgeois in Marxist theory, but a specific figure to be defeated within a given balance of power.

As is the case with the relationship between command and obedience mentioned in the previous chapter, Schmitt's theoretical framework does not serve as a political programme. It should, likewise, not be concluded that politics consists in resorting to the highest level of violence and fear to eradicate one's enemies. Indeed, not all violence is necessarily justifiable or recommendable. Simply put, the issue at hand is to understand why and how politics cannot exist without an enemy, for there is politics only insofar as there is a real or virtual foe. And no self-righteous wishes could ever change anything about it. A people may well declare peace to the whole world, but they will have to take up arms should another people declare war on them instead.

> It would be stupid to believe that a defenceless people could have only friends, just as it would be base and dishonest to expect that one's enemy might allow himself to be moved by non-resistance. The fact that a people no longer has the strength or will to keep itself in the sphere of politics is not the end of world politics. It is merely the end of a weak people. (*The Concept of the Political,* V.)

CHAPTER IV

POLITICAL REALISM — CLARIFICATION

T HIS STUDY OF 'political realism' is far from exhaustive and could still include many chapters on war as a continuation of politics, for example, on the inevitable necessity of 'prejudices' in relation to abstract constructivism, on the importance of decision-making in the creation of a political order, on the dialectic of the private and the public, etc. However, these three detours that focused on Machiavelli, Hobbes and Schmitt serve the function of revealing the presuppositions of politics.

The lessons that we draw from these three authors, however, seem almost banal: is it really surprising to think, through Machiavelli, that politics proceeds in an indefinite space, where no holds are barred, as long as that success is within reach? Is it truly a novelty to state, through Hobbes, that politics revolves around command and obedience above all else? Last but not least, is it revolutionary to see, through Schmitt, that the criterion of friend and foe is the very foundation of all politics? And yet, these are brilliant ideas, in the sense that Gide defined a brilliant idea as a 'superior banality'. When we ponder these affirmations, we acquire the feeling that they are so simple and obvious that any man with the slightest ability to think could have come up with them, but it is actually only at a particular moment in the history of ideas that they reveal themselves to us with power and clairvoyance, for the simple reason that an ingenious man has been able to find the right words to lead us to that point. Ever since the dawn of mankind, we have known that political communities wage war against each other and are more or less consciously prepared for such a possibility. Despite this fact, Carl Schmitt was actually the first to make us aware of the very weight held by this reality and to present us with its conceptual and systematic analysis. What we are referring to here, therefore, are brilliant yet also *original* ideas, in the sense that they take us back to the source of all political action and reflection. Machiavelli, Hobbes and Carl Schmitt complement each other, and the development that takes place through the centuries takes us further and further back, and paradoxically so, to the very origin of things.

Now, the whole point of this *realistic* approach is to be found in the following fact: before becoming a political doctrine, it embodies a method of clarification and intellectual liberation. As previously stated, Machiavelli was not condemned by future generations for his 'immorality'; he was, in fact, condemned for having 'spilled the beans' and for having revealed to us the hypocrisy and ideological attempts to hide politics behind a smokescreen. This is why Julien Freund entreated us to follow his example:

> One must be Machiavellian and be able to recognise the merits of the Florentine's method, and thus be able to reach past the Machiavellianism of many current initiatives that promise either a complete and imminent liberation of man or a radical modification of society. Truth be told, there are some skillful Machiavellians, and others that remain mediocre. For even there, inequality is to be found.[1]

Let us give a specific example to ensure better understanding: the idea of a human society that would be completely unified is an entirely conceivable notion and perhaps even a desirable one in the eyes of certain

---

1   AN: Freund (Julien), *Lettres de la vallée* [TN: Letters from the Valley], Paris, La Nouvelle Librairie, p. 17.

religious or moral systems. Politically, however, mankind appears in the shape of a plurality of political units and heterogeneous groups, and it can readily be expected that this division and separation will persist for as long as man remains man. Of course, it is perfectly admissible for one to dream of the end of this division and, consequently, of the end of all political societies in favour of a purely *moral* one. However, any analysis that does not adopt this division as its starting point is condemned to never understanding the political phenomenon in its essence and, therefore, to failing in its endeavours in a world where one manipulates or is manipulated.

Indeed, since the purpose of the politician lies in the protection of those who obey him, he must, above all, ensure his own success and, to do so, he must take human factors into account, without being diverted away from the latter. If he were to fall prey to the ideals that dreamers and ideologists profess, he would no longer be able to take the reality of man into account and the ground would simply give way beneath his feet. Men can indeed be seized and driven by moral principles, but, just as one does not judge an individual in accordance with the perception he has of himself, one cannot base the safety of a political entity on the ideals it assigns to itself. And this is why capable legislators have always had the wisdom to envision the worst and to assume that man is very easily inclined to commit evil.[2] To use the terms of Max Weber, the politician is driven first and foremost by *the ethics of responsibility*, and therefore by *what is*, while morality is concerned with *what should be*. It can, of course, sometimes happen that the ethics of responsibility and conviction, political action and moral action intersect, but when they come into contradiction, the politician has no choice. Men driven by pure moral will, to the point of refusing to get their hands dirty, are certainly capable of great things and of being genuine inspirations to their fellow men, but they have no *political* vocation. Treitschke notes:

---

2   AN: Hence Machiavelli's maxim according to which the Prince must bear in mind that 'men never do good unless necessity drives them to it'.

> The statesman has no right to warm his hands on the smouldering ruins of his homeland with the convenient satisfaction of saying to himself, "I have never lied", for that is a monk's virtue.[3]

Indeed, he has absolutely no right to do so, because the fate of millions of men depends on his actions, and their fate must matter more to him than his own peace of mind. 'I love my country more than my very soul,'[4] wrote Machiavelli shortly before he died.

This does not mean, however, that political realism is a school of cynicism encouraging its disciples to use extreme and pernicious methods. It is more simply a *habitus*, a frame of mind that must serve as the basis of all authentic political science. The latter must never disregard the fact that both man and human communities are capable of despicable acts, nor must it mask reality in the name of pleasant 'values'. Using Max Weber's *Wertfreiheit* and axiological neutrality, it must rather take into account extreme and exceptional situations just as much as normal ones. And yet, political realism would betray itself by advocating the 'primacy of politics' in all areas of human existence. Indeed, we must not misinterpret things: it would be wrong to say that politics, in itself, takes precedence over aesthetics, morality or spirituality. In this respect, it is simply necessary to state that politics is an autonomous sphere in relation to these other fields of activity. Speaking of the 'primacy of politics' only makes sense insofar as one declares that, in the political domain, what is properly political takes precedence over what is impolitic, that is to say, anything that contradicts the very vocation of politics:

> Therein lies the flaw in purely doctrinal Machiavellianism: it considers existence almost exclusively from the angle of politics, either by ignoring other human activities or by considering them solely as tools of political technique. It arbitrarily gives primacy to politics and, at the same time,

---

3   AN: Treitschke (Heinrich von), *Politik* [TN: Politics] Leipzig, S. Hirzel Verlag, 1899, p. 110.

4   AN: Letter to F. Vettori dated 16 April 1527.

renders itself incapable of grasping its true meaning. Politics can undoubtedly illuminate many aspects of life, but life is not subordinate to it; on
the contrary, it is only possible to grasp the meaning of politics in the
overall context of human existence. Human destiny inevitably transcends
the particularity of political divisions and units. If man cannot understand
himself outside of politics, politics cannot be understood independently of
the human adventure that transcends it.[5]

The role of politics, said Julien Freund, is not to make men better, but
to organise as much as possible the external and collective conditions
that are likely to offer the political unit and the members who live
in it the best prospect of fulfilling what is, or what they individually
consider, to be their vocation. In this sense, politics does not, *in terms
of di*gnity, take primacy over other areas of human existence, but it
must take precedence in the natural order of time and the means em-
ployed. Governing the state is certainly less noble than composing the
Ninth Symphony, but one seldom has the opportunity or the luxury to
compose such a masterpiece when the country is in the grip of chaos
and war. And it is precisely in this manner the Maurrassian maxim
'politics first' illustrates this observation perfectly:[6] prior to being able
to realise their full potential and flourish, men must first ensure the
integrity of their political and social space. That is how one must understand the classic statement according to which the end of politics is
'the common good'. The latter is not the sum of individual 'goods' nor
the good of the state as such, but the good of the entire community
itself to which individual members belong. In other words, it is the
good that men pursue *through shared lives*. If men do indeed live in
political communities, it is because the latter offer them something

---

5   AN: Freund (Julien), *The Essence of the Political, op. cit.*, p. 752.

6   AN: 'When we say "politics first", what we mean to say is that politics comes first
     in the natural order of time and by no means in terms of dignity — just as a road
     must be taken before reaching its end, or as an arrow and a bow must be seized
     before one can strike the target, the means of action will necessarily precede the
     set goal.' (Maurras [Charles], *My Political Ideas,* Paris, Albatros, 1983, p. 155)

that is in their interest, namely *external security* and *internal harmony*. Aristotle was obviously right to think that men exist in society not only to live, but to live well (εὖ ζῆν). Happiness is the very aim of men, all of whom long to lead a good life. And although politics cannot guarantee happiness, its purpose is to provide at least a stable and safe seedbed, an idea that Leibniz expressed with great clarity:

> My definition of the state, or of what the Romans termed *Respublica*, is that it is a large society whose very purpose lies in shared safety. One wishes that one could provide men with something more than security, namely happiness, which one must strive to achieve, but security is, at the very least, essential, for without it *good would cease*.[7]

And this is exactly what the community asks of the politician, namely that he behaves precisely like a politician and thus adapts his actions to the specific goals of the political. He is therefore only blameworthy insofar as he weakens or causes the very ruin of this community, and not if he commits morally questionable acts. *Salus populi suprema lex esto!* Because 'we must not let ourselves be taken in by the legend of the righteous King Saint Louis', Julien Freund reminds us. For even this holy king waged war, undertook crusades, had revolts harshly repressed and abolished various privileges enjoyed by the clergy in the name of the national interest. In short, he acted as a politician. Machiavelli stated:

> Where the safety or interests of the homeland are at stake, there should be no question of reflecting whether a thing is just or unjust, humane or cruel, praiseworthy or shameful. One must take only that course of action which will secure the country's life and liberty.

---

7   AN: Leibniz, *Letter to M. de Falaiseau*, 8 July 1705.

L'INSTITUT ILIADE FOR LONG EUROPEAN MEMORY

L'Institut Iliade for Long European Memory, based in France, was born from an observation. Europe is but a shadow of her former self. Replaced by outsiders, confused by having lost their bearing and their pride, Europeans have abandoned the reins of their common destiny to people other than themselves. Europeans no longer remember. Why? Because amongst the current elite — whether at school, university, or in the media — no one passes down to them the cultural wealth of which they are the inheritors.

Contrary to this moribund current, L'Institut Iliade has given itself the task of participating in the renewal of the cultural grandeur of Europe and in aiding Europeans' reappropriation of their own identity. Facing the Great Erasure of culture, we intend to work for the Great Awakening of European consciousness and to help prepare Europe for a new renaissance — one of identity, freedom, and power.

L'Institut Iliade's calling is threefold:

- To train young men and young women concerned about their history to always build. To make them the avantgarde of the renaissance for which the Institut calls: men and women capable of giving to civic and political action that cultural and metapolitical dimension which is indispensable. Their motto: to put themselves at the service of a community of destiny, which risks disappearing if it is not taken in hand. Armed with a strong culture relating to European traditions and values, they learn to discern that the adventure that awaits them entails risks and self-sacrifice, but also enthusiasm and joy.

- To promote a radical and alternative vision of the world contrary to the dogmas of universalism, egalitarianism, and 'diversity'. Using all available means, the Institut develops concepts and ammunition to understand and fight the modern world.

- To gather together, especially — but not only — in France, those who refuse to submit and who are inspired daily by the Homeric triad as described by Dominique Venner: nature as the base, excellence as the goal, beauty as the horizon.

L'Institut Iliade's originality, especially with the aim of reformulating and updating knowledge, lies in tying together the seriousness of its content with ease of learning for the greater public, the objective being to demonstrate an authentic pedagogy, and to act in complementary or supportive ways with other initiatives having the same goal.

L'Institut Iliade's action takes place across various channels:

- A cadre school of the European Rebirth, which every year brings together trainees from a wide variety of backgrounds and is already seeing citizens from other European countries participate;

- an annual colloquium — made up of academics, politicians, writers, journalists, and association officials from all over Europe — that meets in Paris to discuss strong and challenging themes, such as 'The Aesthetic Universe of Europeans', 'Facing the Migratory Assault', 'Transmit or Disappear', 'Nature as Base — for an Ecology of Place', 'Beyond the Market — Economy at the Service of Peoples';

- the publication of works — designed as beacons to enlighten readers' thoughts and guide them toward the reconquest of their identity — within several collections, made available in the widest array of languages and European countries;

- artistic exhibitions on the fringes of contemporary artistic trends, allowing the public to take a fresh look at art and rooted creation;

- an incubator for ideas, businesses, and associations to support and help the greatest number of projects — with quality and sustainability criteria — across all fields of civil society (culture, commerce, etc.) that seek to impose a rooted vision of the world and an alternative to the current system, while prioritising structures and projects making an impact in real life;

- an active presence on social media, allowing us to reach new audiences (through videos, publications, annual events, and news presentations), centred around a website that functions as much as a resource hub as it does as a platform for exchanges and debate, notably offering an ideal library of more than five hundred works, a European primer, a dictionary of quotations, and turnkey itineraries for visiting and hiking the prominent places of European memory.

Education through history:

L'Institut Iliade endeavours to uphold in every circumstance the richness and singularity of our heritage in order to draw forth the source and the resources of a serene, but determined, affirmation of our identity, both national and European. In line with the thought and deeds of Dominique Venner, the Institut accords in all its activities an essential place to history, both as a matrix of deep meditation on the future as well as a place of the unexpected, where anything is possible.

C ONCERNING EUROPE, it seems as though we will be forced to rise up and face immense challenges and fearsome catastrophes even beyond those posed by immigration. These hardships will present the opportunity for both a rebirth and a rediscovery of ourselves. I believe in those qualities that are specific to the European people, qualities currently in a state of dormancy. I believe in our active individuality, our inventiveness, and in the awakening of our energy. This awakening will undoubtedly come. When? I do not know, but I am positive that it will take place.

— DOMINIQUE VENNER, *The Shock of History*
Arktos Media, London, 2015

Follow L'Institut Iliade at
www.institut-iliade.com
linktr.ee/InstitutILIADE

OTHER BOOKS PUBLISHED BY ARKTOS

	The Myth of the Blood
	Notes on the Third Reich
	Pagan Imperialism
	Recognitions
	A Traditionalist Confronts Fascism
GUILLAUME FAYE	*Archeofuturism*
	Archeofuturism 2.0
	The Colonisation of Europe
	Convergence of Catastrophes
	Ethnic Apocalypse
	A Global Coup
	Prelude to War
	Sex and Deviance
	Understanding Islam
	Why We Fight
DANIEL S. FORREST	*Suprahumanism*
ANDREW FRASER	*Dissident Dispatches*
	Reinventing Aristocracy in the Age of Woke Capital
	The WASP Question
GÉNÉRATION IDENTITAIRE	*We are Generation Identity*
PETER GOODCHILD	*The Taxi Driver from Baghdad*
	The Western Path
PAUL GOTTFRIED	*War and Democracy*
PETR HAMPL	*Breached Enclosure*
PORUS HOMI HAVEWALA	*The Saga of the Aryan Race*
CONSTANTIN VON HOFFMEISTER	*Esoteric Trumpism*
	MULTIPOLARITY!
RICHARD HOUCK	*Liberalism Unmasked*
A. J. ILLINGWORTH	*Political Justice*
INSTITUT ILIADE	*For a European Awakening*
	Guardians of Heritage
ALEXANDER JACOB	*De Naturae Natura*
JASON REZA JORJANI	*Artemis Unveiled*
	Closer Encounters
	Erosophia
	Faustian Futurist
	Iranian Leviathan
	Lovers of Sophia
	Metapolemos
	Novel Folklore
	Philosophy of the Future
	Prometheism
	Promethean Pirate
	Prometheus and Atlas
	Psychotron
	Uber Man
	World State of Emergency
HENRIK JONASSON	*Sigmund*

OTHER BOOKS PUBLISHED BY ARKTOS

OTHER BOOKS PUBLISHED BY ARKTOS